Though she be but little, she is fierce.

— Shakespeare

This above all: to thine ownself be true.

– Shakespeare

Excellence is not an act, but a habit.

– Aristotle

No act of kindness, no matter how small, is
ever wasted.

- Aesop

The way to be happy is to make others so.

— Robert Ingersoll

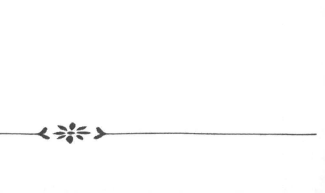

She is clothed in strength and
dignity and she laughs without fear
of the future.

— Proverbs 31:25 KJV

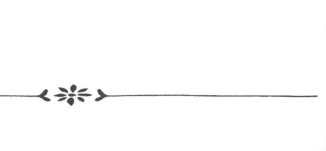

Peace is always beautiful.

— Walt Whitman

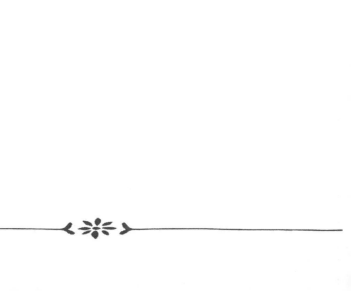

I am not bothered by the fact that I am
not understood.

— Confucius

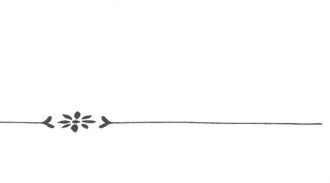

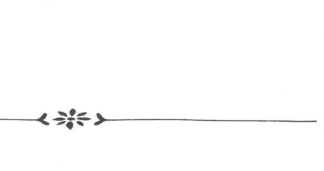

Bloom where you are planted.

- 1 Corinthians KJV

Made in the USA
San Bernardino, CA
27 April 2019